DEADLY DISEASES

COVID-19

BY CAROL HAND

CONTENT CONSULTANT
Kevin M. Bakker
Assistant Research Scientist, Department of Epidemiology
School of Public Health, University of Michigan

Cover image: The virus that causes COVID-19 has distinctive spikes around its outer surface.

Core Library
An Imprint of Abdo Publishing
abdobooks.com

abdobooks.com

Published by Abdo Publishing, a division of ABDO, PO Box 398166, Minneapolis, Minnesota 55439.

Printed in the United States of America, North Mankato, Minnesota.
102021
012022

THIS BOOK CONTAINS RECYCLED MATERIALS

Cover Photo: Shutterstock Images
Interior Photos: Sasirin Pamai/Shutterstock Images, 4–5; Shutterstock Images, 6, 14–15, 18, 19, 25, 27, 43; Darren Baker/Shutterstock Images, 10; FeatureChina/AP Images, 20; Science Photo Library/Science Source, 22–23, 45; Alexandros Michailidis/Shutterstock Images, 30–31; Laurie A. Smith/Shutterstock Images, 33; Marian Weyo/Shutterstock Images, 35; Carolyn Kaster/AP Images, 37; Fotogramma/Reda & Co/UIG/Science Source, 40

Editor: Arnold Ringstad
Series Designer: Ryan Gale

Library of Congress Control Number: 2021941236

Publisher's Cataloging-in-Publication Data

Names: Hand, Carol, author.
Title: COVID-19 / by Carol Hand
Description: Minneapolis, Minnesota : Abdo Publishing, 2022 | Series: Deadly diseases | Includes online resources and index.
Identifiers: ISBN 9781532196577 (lib. bdg.) | ISBN 9781098218386 (ebook)
Subjects: LCSH: COVID-19 (Disease)--Juvenile literature. | Coronaviruses--Juvenile literature. | Infectious diseases--Juvenile literature. | Epidemics--History--Juvenile literature. | Communicable diseases--Epidemiology--Juvenile literature.
Classification: DDC 614.49--dc23

CONTENTS

CHAPTER ONE
What Is COVID-19? 4

CHAPTER TWO
The History of COVID-19 14

CHAPTER THREE
The Science of COVID-19 22

CHAPTER FOUR
Treating COVID-19 30

Important Dates 42

Stop and Think 44

Glossary 46

Online Resources 47

Learn More 47

Index 48

About the Author 48

CHAPTER ONE

WHAT IS COVID-19?

Antonio and Estelita Solomon were born in the Philippines. They both immigrated to the United States to find a better life. Antonio served in the US Navy for more than two decades. He later worked for the postal service. Estelita worked as a nurse in New York City for 36 years. They had two daughters, Cathrine and EmyLou. In early 2020, Antonio and Estelita were living in retirement when the COVID-19 pandemic began.

The COVID-19 pandemic isolated, sickened, and killed millions of people around the world.

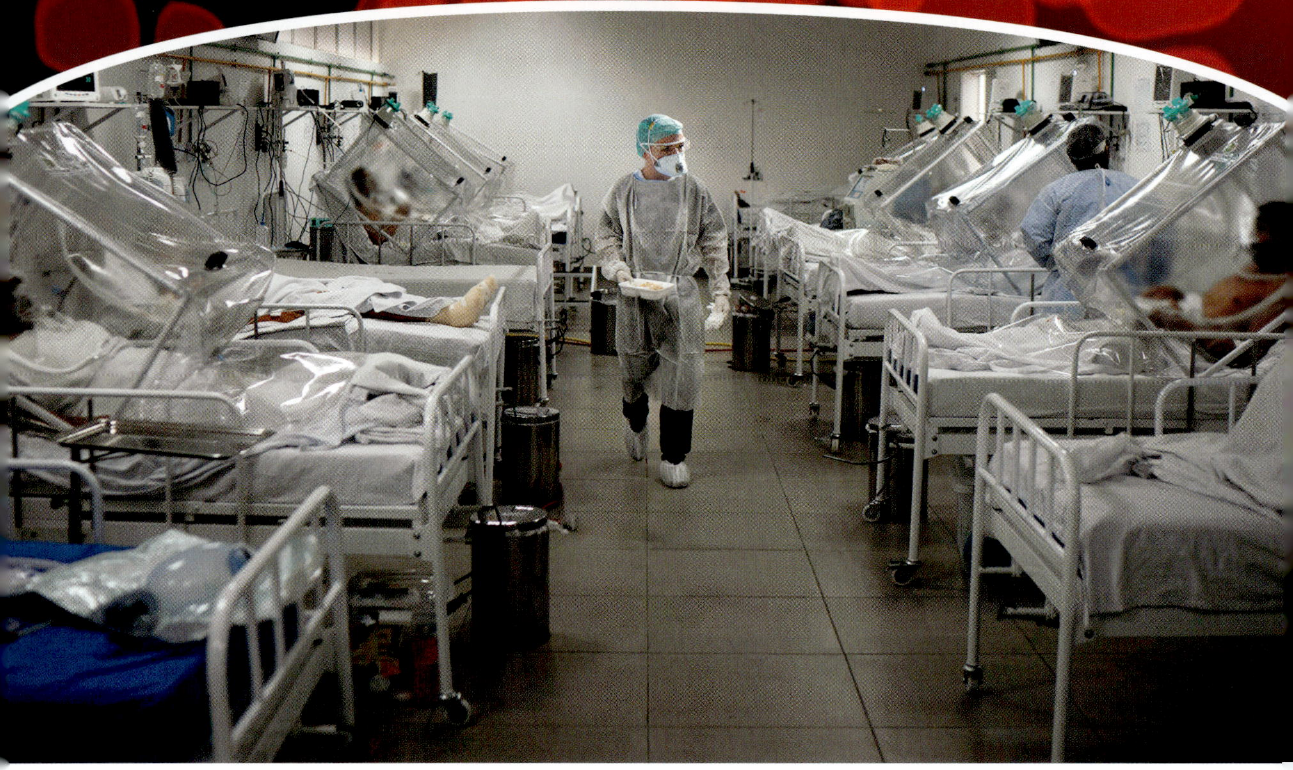

The deadly COVID-19 pandemic took a huge toll on countries around the world.

Both of them caught the disease in the spring of 2020. Antonio died on March 26. On April 10, Estelita died too. Cathrine and EmyLou had lost both their parents in the span of two weeks. But their pain was not over yet. Their uncle, Antonio's brother, died of COVID-19 on April 17. EmyLou told reporters, "We were expecting my parents to live out a long, fulfilling life. And if it wasn't for COVID, they would still be here today. Their life was cut short."

BREAKING FAMILIES APART

The Solomon family's experience was not unique. It was repeated thousands of times across the country. Kelly Styers of Michigan lost her mother, father, and brother. Erika Martinez of California lost her father and brother. Within a year of the pandemic starting, the disease killed more than 500,000 Americans. Each death from COVID-19 created a hole in a family. These people were parents, grandparents, spouses, children, and cousins.

When people have severe COVID-19, they may be isolated in the hospital. Doctors don't want them to spread the disease. Family members can't visit. This means many patients suffer and die without their loved ones nearby.

After a person dies, family members want to grieve for them. This may mean holding a funeral. But the pandemic was still going on. People had to be careful

PERSPECTIVES

TEACHERS AND THE PANDEMIC

The COVID-19 pandemic has been hard on teachers. Many were not prepared to teach online. They also worried for their students' well-being. Teacher Beth Grounds reflected after a year of teaching remotely: "I believe that there's a certain magic that happens in the classroom when you have 24 students of differing backgrounds and cultures that get together. They learn so much just from the face-to-face communication. They learn how to share. . . . to compromise. They laugh. . . . This was not a situation that any of us wanted, but we did try to make the best of it."

about gathering in large groups. They didn't want to catch the disease. Funerals were changed or delayed. This made things especially hard for families.

It can be hard to imagine the deaths of hundreds of thousands of people. Cathrine Solomon told reporters that her parents were more than statistics. She said, "Our parents were [not] just numbers. They were real people with good lives, who had so much life in them."

THE BASICS OF COVID-19

COVID-19 is a disease caused by a virus. The virus belongs to a family of viruses called coronaviruses. Different coronaviruses cause different respiratory diseases. These diseases affect the lungs and airways. Some coronaviruses cause colds and flus, which usually last only a few days to a week.

VIRUSES AND CORONAVIRUSES

A virus consists of a piece of genetic material surrounded by a protein coat. Viruses are not considered to be alive. They cannot reproduce on their own. Instead, they invade living cells and use the cells' materials to reproduce. This process causes disease. Coronaviruses are a family of viruses that affect the lungs. *Corona* means "crown." These viruses are round. Their surfaces are covered with crown-like spikes.

COVID-19 varies widely from person to person. Some people have no symptoms at all. Some have a

mild illness similar to the flu. But some have trouble breathing. Some patients' lungs fail, and they die. Those who survive may suffer lasting damage to their heart, lungs, nervous system, or kidneys. People may lose their sense of smell or taste. They may experience feelings of weakness.

COVID-19 is spread by droplets released by an infected person. When that person breathes, talks, laughs, coughs, or sneezes, droplets containing virus particles enter the air. People nearby may breathe in those particles. This happens most easily in crowded and indoor spaces. To slow the spread, people can wear masks and practice social distancing. This means staying at least six feet (1.8 m) from each other.

In rare cases, surface contact can spread the disease. Droplets that contain the virus may land on objects or surfaces. If a person touches the surface and

People around the world wore masks to help slow the spread of COVID-19.

then his or her eyes, nose, or mouth, that person may become infected.

The pandemic changed lives around the world in early 2020. Nearly everyone was affected by COVID-19 in some way. Many kids started doing school online. Some adults started working from home. Many others had to keep going to their jobs. Their work could not be done remotely. These people included health-care workers, grocery store clerks, and others. People across the globe took steps to stay safe. But COVID-19 still spread like wildfire. Tens of millions of people were infected. Tragically, like the Solomons, many lost their lives.

STRAIGHT TO THE SOURCE

The Centers for Disease Control and Prevention (CDC) is a US government agency. The people at the CDC work to protect the nation's health. The CDC issued guidelines for wearing face masks to slow the spread of COVID-19:

> *CDC recommends that people wear masks in public settings, at events and gatherings, and anywhere they will be around other people. When you wear a mask, you protect others as well as yourself. Masks work best when everyone wears one. A mask is NOT a substitute for social distancing. Masks should still be worn in addition to staying at least 6 feet apart, especially when indoors around people who don't live in your household.*

Source: "Guidance for Wearing Masks." *CDC*, 19 Apr. 2021, cdc.gov. Accessed 1 July 2021.

WHAT'S THE BIG IDEA?

Read the passage above. What is its main idea? Give at least two details from the passage that support the main idea.

CHAPTER
TWO

THE HISTORY OF COVID-19

The first known case of COVID-19 was reported on December 1, 2019, in Wuhan, a city in central China. Scientists identified the virus that causes the disease. They named it SARS-CoV-2. The disease is very contagious. It spread easily through Wuhan, which is a highly populated and transient city. Then it started to spread throughout the world. The World Health Organization (WHO) declared COVID-19 a pandemic on March 11, 2020.

Early cases of COVID-19 were reported in Wuhan, China, but the disease soon spread across the globe.

WHERE COVID-19 CAME FROM

Coronaviruses are often found in animals such as cattle. Rarely, a coronavirus moves to humans. This probably happened with SARS-CoV-2. No one yet knows exactly how it spread to people. Most scientists believe the virus started in bats, jumped to another animal, and then entered humans. Reports trace some of the earliest cases back to markets in Wuhan. More research is needed to be sure.

COVID-19 spreads rapidly from person to person. The closer together people are, the more likely they are to spread it. The incubation period for a virus is how long it takes an infected person to show symptoms.

EPIDEMICS AND PANDEMICS

An epidemic occurs when there is a sudden large increase in cases of a disease. It may have been introduced into a new area. Or it may have changed to be able to spread more easily. If the increase is limited to a small geographic area, it is called an outbreak. If the disease spreads over several continents, it becomes a pandemic.

For SARS-CoV-2, it ranges from two to fourteen days. The median time is five days. An infected person is most contagious when he or she has symptoms. But infections can also be spread by people who carry the virus and have no symptoms.

COVID-19 CONTROL IN CHINA

The COVID-19 pandemic started in China. The country took steps to control it. On January 23, 2020, Wuhan was locked down. But by that time, at least 5 million people had traveled out of the city.

Wuhan's lockdown lasted 76 days. There

PERSPECTIVES

IMPACT ON ASIAN COMMUNITIES

The SARS-CoV-2 virus was first seen in China. Many people wrongly blamed Asian communities for the pandemic. They began attacking people of Asian descent online, in the media, and in real life. Violent attacks against Asian Americans rose sharply. Local governments and anti-hate groups began taking action against this discrimination and violence.

Nursing home residents around the world faced particular danger from COVID-19.

were no large gatherings. Family members could leave the house only every few days to collect supplies. The government tested people for the virus and traced their contacts. People wore face masks. Experts estimated that China's quick response, which used lessons from past outbreaks, may have prevented 1.4 million infections and 56,000 deaths.

China's government has strict control over its people. In Europe and the United States, people were

COVID-19'S

US DEATH TOLL

The first confirmed death from COVID-19 in the United States happened on February 6, 2020. It took more than three months for the death toll to reach 100,000. Four months after that, it topped 200,000. It rapidly climbed over the next few months before slowing after vaccines rolled out in the spring of 2021. How does this calendar help you better understand the timeline of the COVID-19 pandemic in the United States?

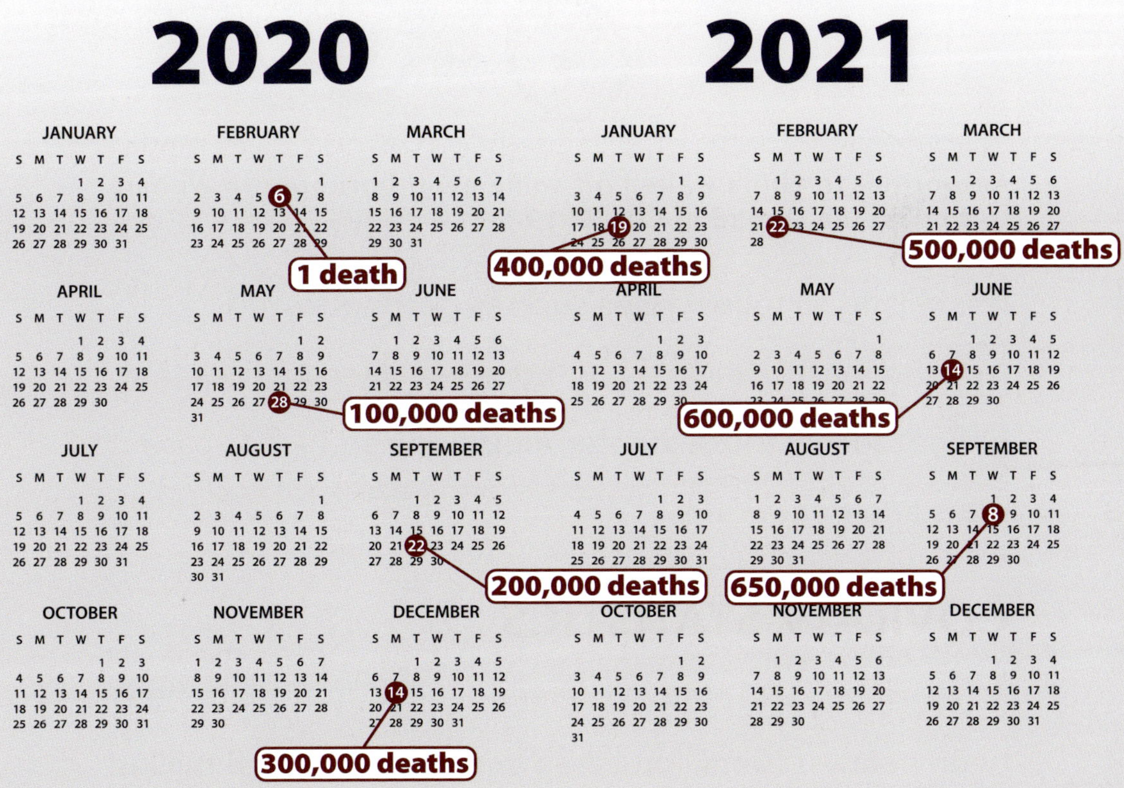

Authorities in China walled off some neighborhoods in Wuhan to control the spread of COVID-19.

less willing to follow rules such as getting tested, wearing masks, and staying home. Many countries that did not follow these stricter methods had higher case rates and death rates.

COVID-19 STATISTICS

In late June 2021, the WHO announced that there had been nearly 180 million cases and more than 3.8 million deaths worldwide. In the United States during the same time period, there had been about 34 million cases and 620,000 deaths.

Hope for ending the pandemic lay in the vaccines that scientists developed in 2020. By June 2021, more than 2.4 billion doses had been given around the world. Some of the vaccines required two doses. That means that the number of people fully vaccinated was less than 2.4 billion. Countries raced to vaccinate more people to stop the spread of COVID-19.

FURTHER EVIDENCE

Chapter Two discusses the early history of the COVID-19 pandemic. What was one of the main points of the chapter? What are some pieces of evidence used to support that point? Read the article at the website below. Does the information on the website support the main point of the chapter? Does it present new information?

NPR: THE ORIGINS OF COVID-19?

abdocorelibrary.com/covid-19

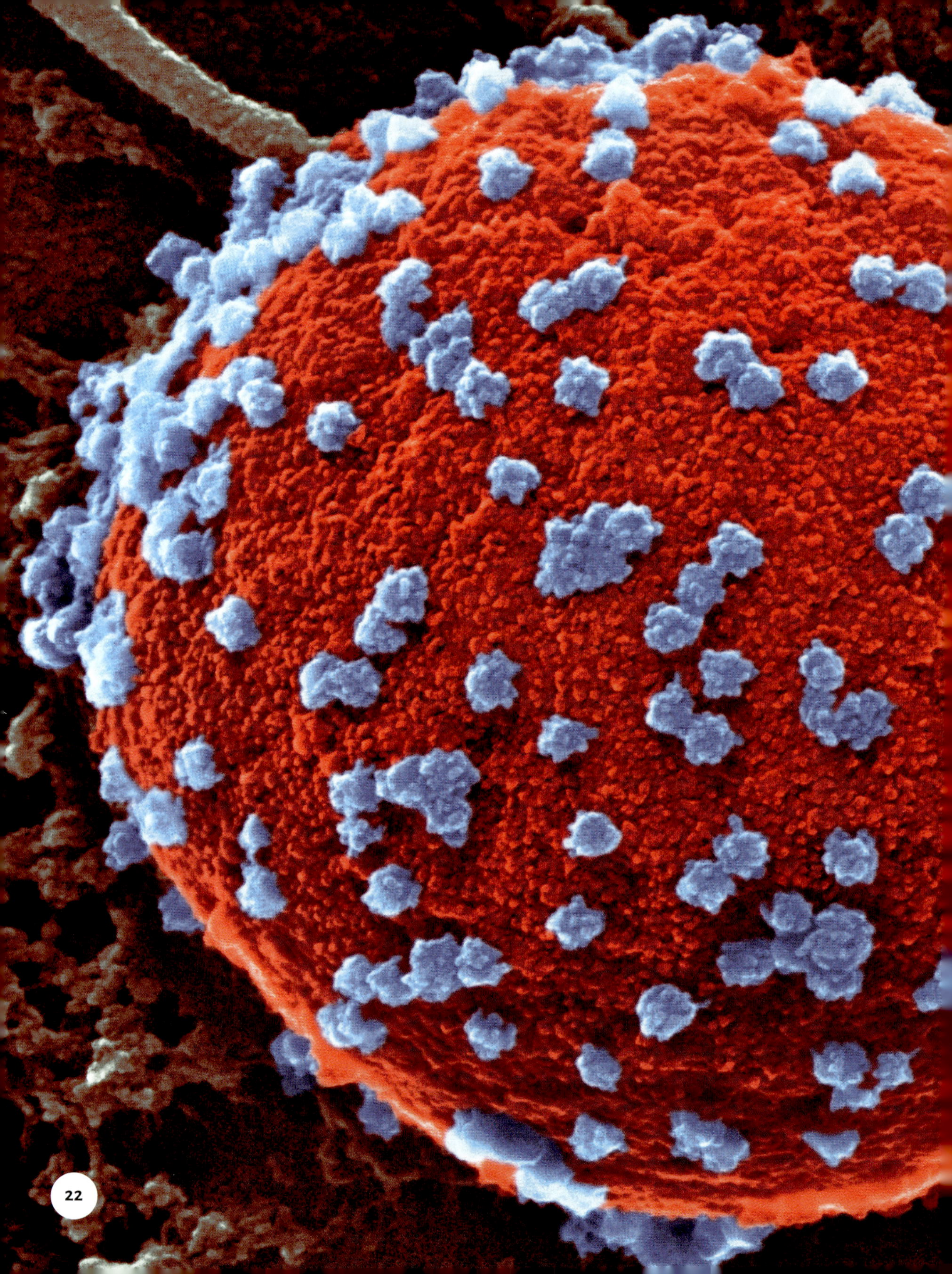

CHAPTER THREE

THE SCIENCE OF COVID-19

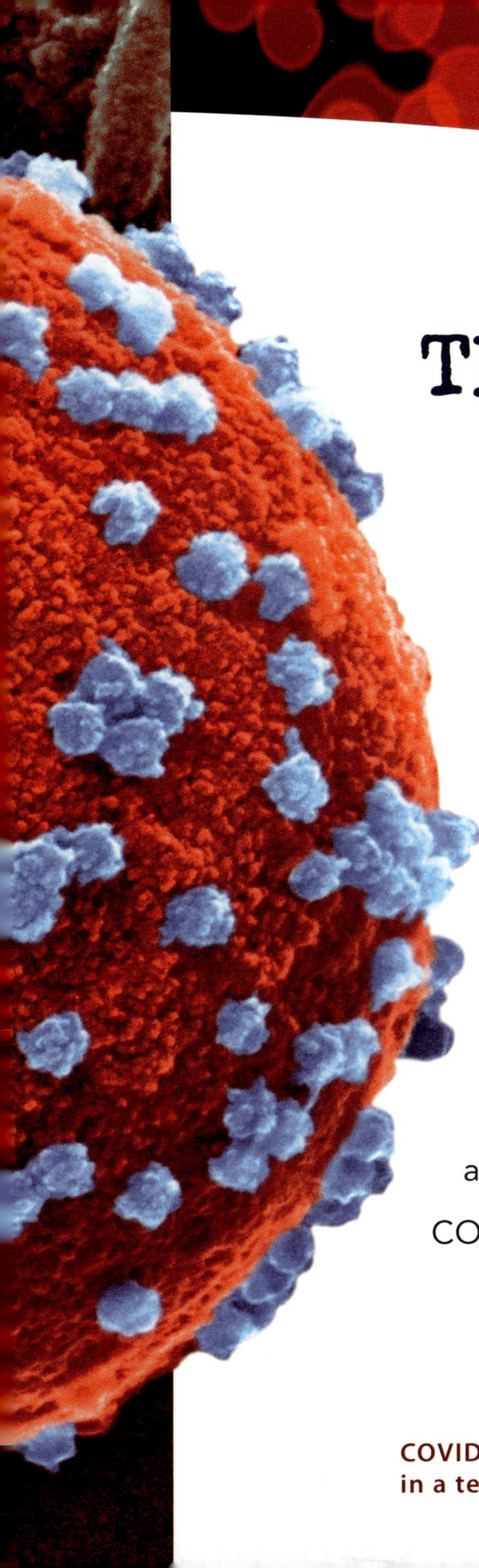

Several serious pandemics have been caused by viruses jumping from animals to humans. Both the 1918 and 2009 H1N1 influenza pandemics started in pigs. Ebola started in bats. MERS probably started in bats but was transmitted to humans by camels. SARS and COVID-19 are likely from bats too. MERS, SARS, and COVID-19 are all coronaviruses.

COVID-19 virus particles, *blue*, attack a cell, *red*, in a test carried out in a laboratory.

WHO IS AT RISK?

Anyone can get COVID-19. But not everyone is equally likely to get severely ill or die from it. Certain groups, especially elderly people, are at much higher risk. More than 80 percent of deaths occur in people age 65 and older. More than 95 percent occur in those over 45. Many people in racial and ethnic minority groups are at higher risk. Communities with large minority populations saw higher death rates from COVID-19. This is mainly due to long-term social and health inequities that contribute to more preexisting health conditions.

HOW VIRUSES SPREAD

Different pandemic viruses are spread in different ways. All coronaviruses, including SARS-CoV-2, spread through respiratory droplets. These droplets are created when people cough, sneeze, sing, or talk. Avian influenza spreads by contact with infected poultry. Ebola spreads by contact with infected blood or bodily fluids.

Elderly people faced higher risks than younger individuals from COVID-19.

People with chronic medical conditions are at higher risk than healthy people of any age. This includes people with heart, lung, kidney, or liver disease. It also includes those with diabetes, cancer, HIV infection, and weakened immune systems. People with obesity, pregnant women, and smokers have a higher risk too.

Children and teens can also get COVID-19. Some develop severe cases. A few even die. But these outcomes are rare. The kids and teens most at risk for severe illness from COVID-19 are those with chronic conditions. The conditions causing risk are the same in children and adults. Children are best protected from COVID-19 when all adults in the household are fully vaccinated.

HOW VIRUSES INVADE CELLS

A virus works by entering a living cell and taking over its functions. It forces the cell to build new copies of the virus.

People mainly get COVID-19 by breathing in SARS-CoV-2 particles. The crown-like spikes on the virus are proteins that help it invade cells. The virus attaches to cells, mostly in the lungs. Then it enters the cells.

Inside cells, the virus's genetic material goes to the cell nucleus. This genetic material is called RNA. The RNA makes copies of itself. The copies leave the

HOW SARS-COV-2 INVADES CELLS

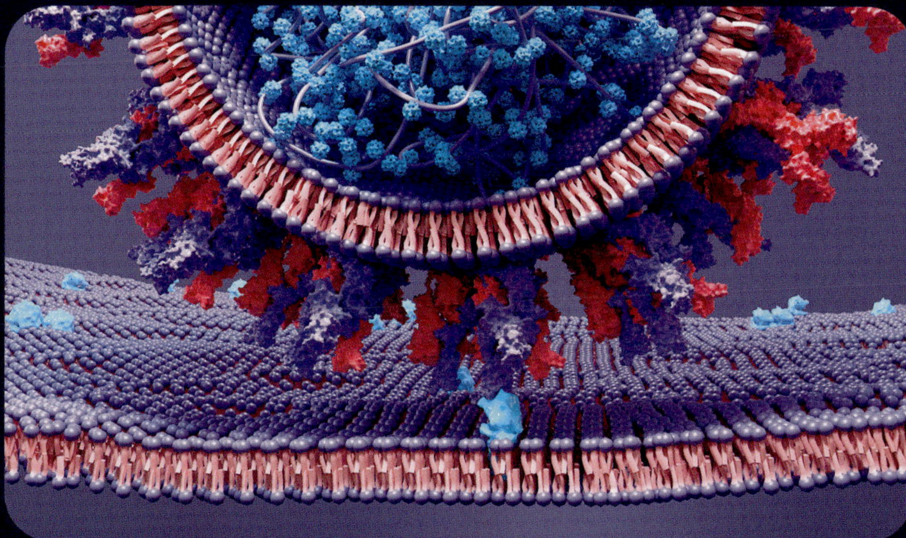

The outer proteins, or spikes, of the SARS-CoV-2 virus attach to living cells. This image shows how the spike protein connects to the outer wall of a cell. How does this diagram help you better understand how the virus invades cells?

nucleus and are coated with protein molecules. Each cell makes millions of copies of the virus. These copies enter other healthy cells and multiply again. As more cells are affected, the disease becomes more serious.

SYMPTOMS OF COVID-19

Not everyone who becomes infected with SARS-CoV-2 experiences the symptoms of COVID-19. But many do. These symptoms include shortness of breath, a persistent cough, and pain and tightness in the chest. Other symptoms include fever, fatigue, and loss of the senses of smell and taste. Most people with these symptoms, about 80 percent, recover within two weeks without medical treatment.

But in some people, the virus seriously affects the lungs. These people have trouble breathing.

PERSPECTIVES

COVID-19 LONG HAULERS

Sometimes COVID-19 symptoms last for many weeks or months. People in this situation have become known as COVID-19 long haulers. Even after they test negative for the virus, they remain ill. Some have the original symptoms. Others develop new symptoms. The most common symptoms of long haulers include fatigue, coughing, body aches, and joint pain. Shortness of breath, loss of smell and taste, sleeping problems, headaches, and difficulty concentrating are also common. Because COVID-19 is so new, little is known about how long this condition will last or how serious it is.

Their levels of blood oxygen become low. They may develop pneumonia or fluid in the lungs. If the symptoms become too severe, patients may be placed on a breathing tube or ventilator to help them breathe. This can cause lung injuries. The disease can also harm other body systems. These include the blood, kidneys, brain and nervous system, cardiovascular system, and gastrointestinal system.

EXPLORE ONLINE

Chapter Three discusses how the virus that causes COVID-19 affects the body. The website below talks more about the virus. Does the website answer any more questions you have about COVID-19?

MAYO CLINIC: COVID-19

abdocorelibrary.com/covid-19

CHAPTER FOUR

TREATING COVID-19

When the COVID-19 pandemic started, people knew nothing about the virus. Scientists studied it as the disease spread. Findings have often been confusing. Experts and leaders based their actions partly on past pandemics. They made their best guesses as they learned more about SARS-CoV-2.

Scientists and doctors have gained a better understanding of COVID-19. But its long-term effects remain unclear. In addition, viruses have the ability to mutate, or change.

Health-care workers had to quickly learn the best ways to treat patients with COVID-19.

This can make it more difficult to treat and prevent the spread of COVID-19 in the future.

PREVENTIVE MEASURES

The best way to deal with any pandemic is to prevent people from getting the disease. When fewer people are infected, the disease spreads more slowly. Eventually it will slow and stop. Before vaccines were available, preventive measures were the only way to stay safe from COVID-19. Even as vaccines became more widely available, preventive measures remained important.

PERSPECTIVES

CHANGING GUIDELINES

CDC guidelines continued to change as more people were vaccinated for COVID-19. In April 2021, the CDC stated that fully vaccinated people need not wear masks outdoors except in crowds. They could go to work after exposure to COVID-19 if they had no symptoms. In May 2021, the CDC said that people who were vaccinated could stop wearing masks indoors, too.

Closing places where people gathered closely together, such as movie theaters, was one way communities fought the pandemic.

Some people were too young to receive a vaccine, and others chose not to.

During the worst of the pandemic, many US states and other countries went on lockdown to slow COVID-19. Governments imposed curfews and travel restrictions. They made laws to limit large gatherings. They closed gyms and restaurant dining rooms. Sporting events were canceled. Schools were closed, and students took online classes. Many people worked online from home. A study published about seven months after the pandemic began showed that lockdowns were highly effective in preventing the virus from spreading.

TREATMENTS

Most COVID-19 cases are mild and can be treated at home. The patient should stay in a separate room from other family members. If possible, the person should have a separate bathroom. Patients should treat the symptoms of the virus as they would the flu. This means taking cough medicine and using acetaminophen for fevers. People should consume warm drinks such as tea or broth to stay hydrated. They can practice relaxation techniques and breathing slowly to help with shortness of breath.

For many patients with mild cases of COVID-19, resting at home is the best treatment.

Patients with moderate COVID-19 have lung infections. These patients should be monitored closely in the hospital. Doctors may give them antibiotics to kill any bacterial infections. Moderate cases can quickly become severe if oxygen levels drop and respiratory rates increase. Patients are then given oxygen. In severe or critical cases, they are placed on a ventilator to aid breathing. They will likely be admitted to an intensive care unit (ICU).

VACCINES

The only way to truly control a pandemic such as COVID-19 is to develop vaccines against it. A vaccine is given before a person gets sick. It prevents infection rather than treating it. But vaccine development takes a long time. Most vaccines take ten to fifteen years to develop. Before 2020, the mumps vaccine was the fastest vaccine to be developed. It became available in 1967 after four years of work.

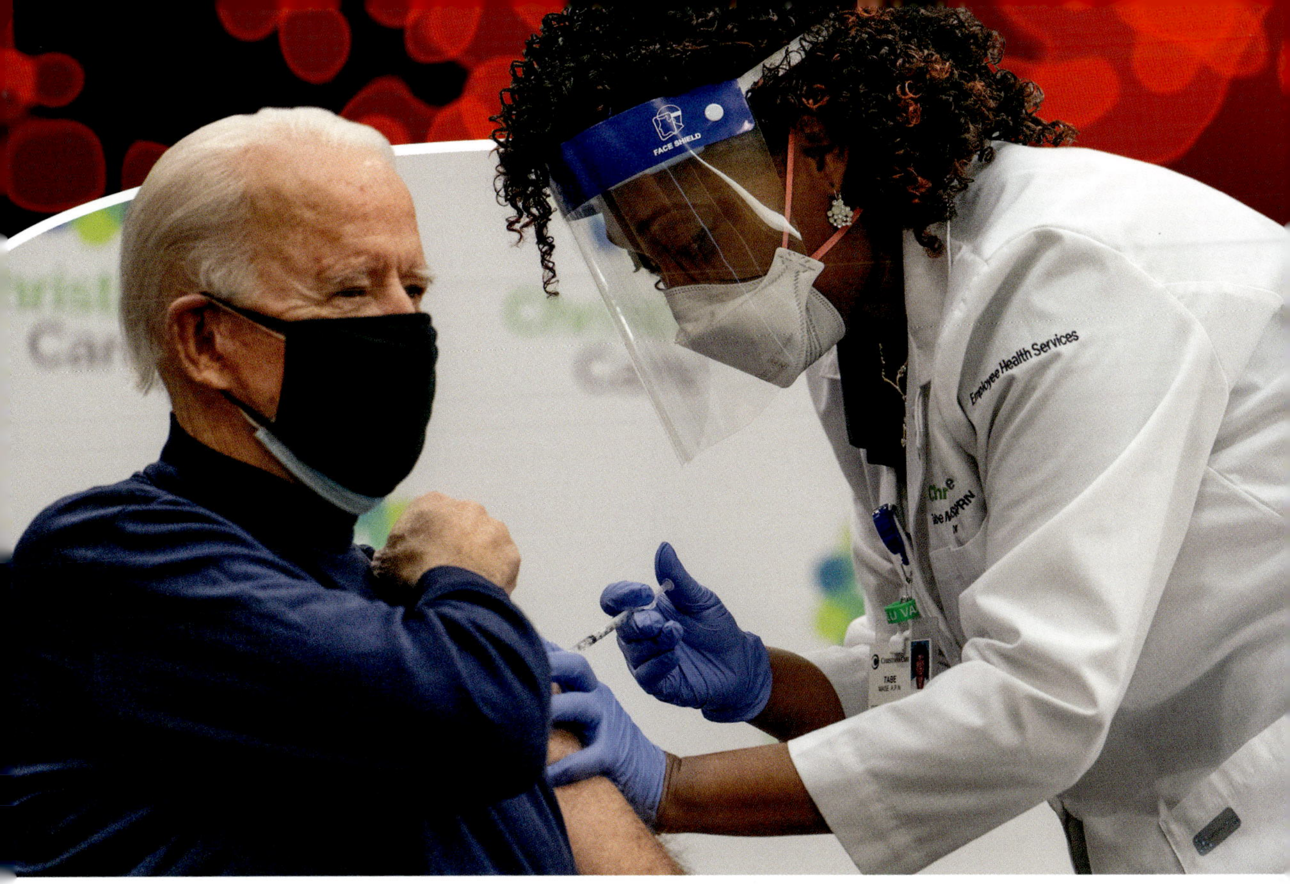

President Joe Biden and other officials were vaccinated publicly to help encourage others to get their shots.

When most of a population is immune to a disease, the entire population is indirectly protected. This is called herd immunity. Having large numbers of immune people means that encountering an infected person is unlikely. This controls the spread of the disease. A higher vaccination rate provides greater protection.

To prevent more people from dying, the US Department of Health and Human Services (HHS) began

Operation Warp Speed (OWS). The program provided money to drug companies researching the vaccines. Scientists worked efficiently to develop several safe and effective vaccines that prevent COVID-19.

TYPES OF VACCINES

By late April 2021, three different vaccines were available to adults in the United States. The CDC considered all three vaccines safe and effective. It found that they reduced the risk of severe illness from COVID-19. It recommended that people take whichever vaccine was available. Two of the vaccines, Pfizer-BioNTech and Moderna, required two doses to be effective. The third, Johnson & Johnson's Janssen vaccine, required a single dose.

The first US vaccination was given on December 14, 2020, to an ICU nurse in a New York hospital. It had been less than nine months since OWS began. By June 2021, more than 150 million people in the United States were fully vaccinated.

LOOKING AHEAD

Viruses are constantly changing as they spread. This process is called mutation. It involves slight changes in the virus's genetic material. In the case of COVID-19, mutations often change the spike proteins that help the virus attach to cells. The mutated viruses are called variants. They may change how the virus spreads or how it affects people.

By June 2021, at least six potentially serious COVID-19 variants were spreading in the United States. One was first identified in the United Kingdom. It appeared in the United States in late 2020. Others were first identified in South Africa, Brazil, and California. The names of the variants were later given Greek letters to avoid linking them to specific countries. For example, they included the alpha, beta, and delta variants. Some variants were able to spread faster than the original virus. Scientists found that some vaccines were still effective against these mutations. But they watched closely for the rise of any dangerous new variants.

Scientists raced to learn more about the virus and find ways to beat the pandemic.

The COVID-19 pandemic changed the world. The virus killed millions of people, and it infected millions more. Lockdowns led to businesses closing and people losing jobs. But the pandemic also showed the power of science. Researchers quickly learned about the virus. They developed safe and effective vaccines in record time. Scientists hoped the lessons they learned would help the world be more ready for the next pandemic.

STRAIGHT TO THE SOURCE

The process of vaccine development was changed for COVID-19 vaccines. These changes are discussed in the following post from the CDC:

> *New vaccines are first developed in laboratories. . . . After initial development, vaccines go through three phases of clinical trials to make sure they are safe and effective. For other vaccines . . . the three phases of clinical trials are performed one at a time. During the development of COVID-19 vaccines, these phases have overlapped to speed up the process so the vaccines can be used as quickly as possible to control the pandemic. No trial phases have been skipped. The clinical trials for COVID-19 vaccines have involved tens of thousands of volunteers. . . . Results from these trials have shown that COVID-19 vaccines are effective.*

Source: "Developing COVID-19 Vaccines." *CDC*, 25 Mar. 2021, cdc.gov. Accessed 11 June 2021.

BACK IT UP

In this text, the CDC is using evidence to make a point. Write a paragraph describing the point. Then list two or three pieces of evidence used to make the point.

IMPORTANT DATES

2019
The first case of a new coronavirus, later named SARS-CoV-2, is reported in Wuhan, China, in December. It causes a dangerous illness named COVID-19.

2020
In January the Chinese government sets up a country-wide lockdown for 76 days. The lockdown succeeds in slowing the spread of COVID-19.

2020
On March 11, the World Health Organization (WHO) declares COVID-19 a pandemic.

2020
On March 30, the US Department of Health and Human Services (HHS) begins Operation Warp Speed (OWS) to speed up vaccine development.

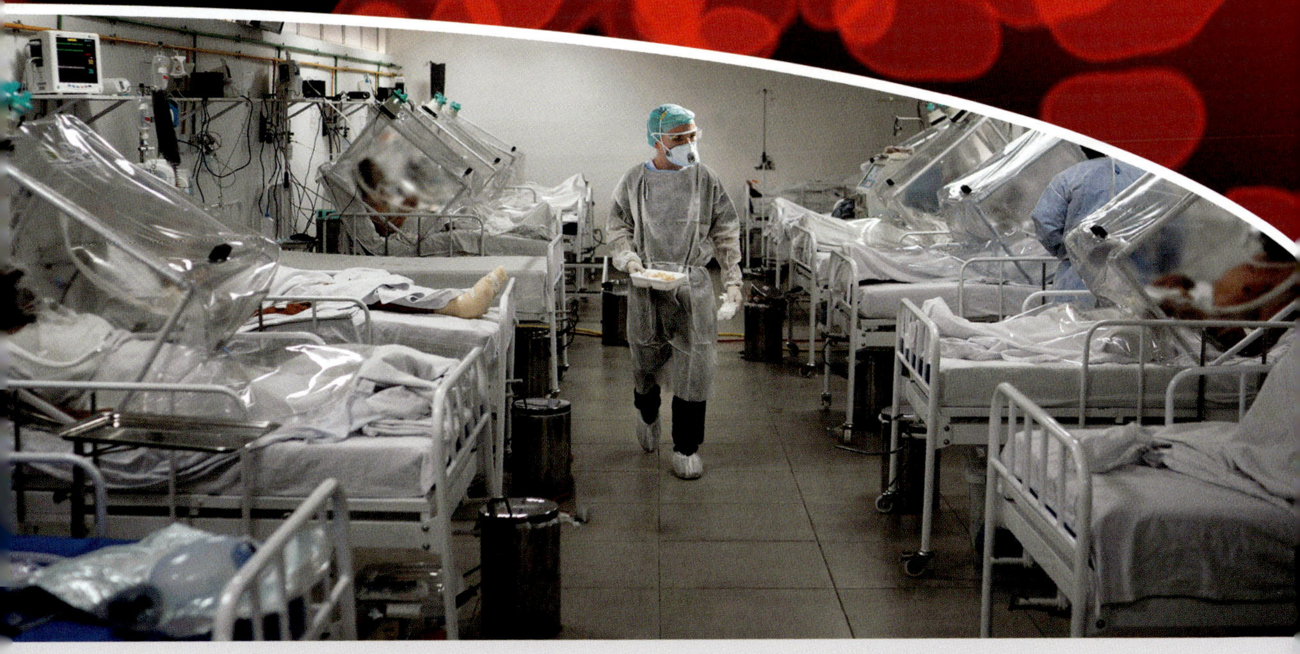

2020

In December, a new COVID variant first identified in the United Kingdom is found in the United States. It begins spreading faster than the original virus.

2020

The first US COVID-19 vaccination is given to a nurse in New York City on December 14.

2021

In February the number of COVID-19–related deaths in the United States reaches 500,000.

2021

By June, six potentially serious variants of the virus causing COVID-19 have been identified and are spreading in the United States.

STOP AND THINK

Tell the Tale

Chapter One discusses the tragedies experienced by people during the COVID-19 pandemic. Write 200 words about your own experience during the pandemic. Were you in lockdown? What was it like? How did it make you feel? What did you give up during that time?

Surprise Me

After reading about the history of COVID-19 in Chapter Two, list several things that surprised you about its origin. Write two or three sentences about each fact. Why did you find each fact surprising?

Why Do I Care?

Most young people are at a low risk for severe illness due to COVID-19. Do you think young people still have a responsibility to take precautions, such as wearing a mask? How might this decision affect other people in a community?

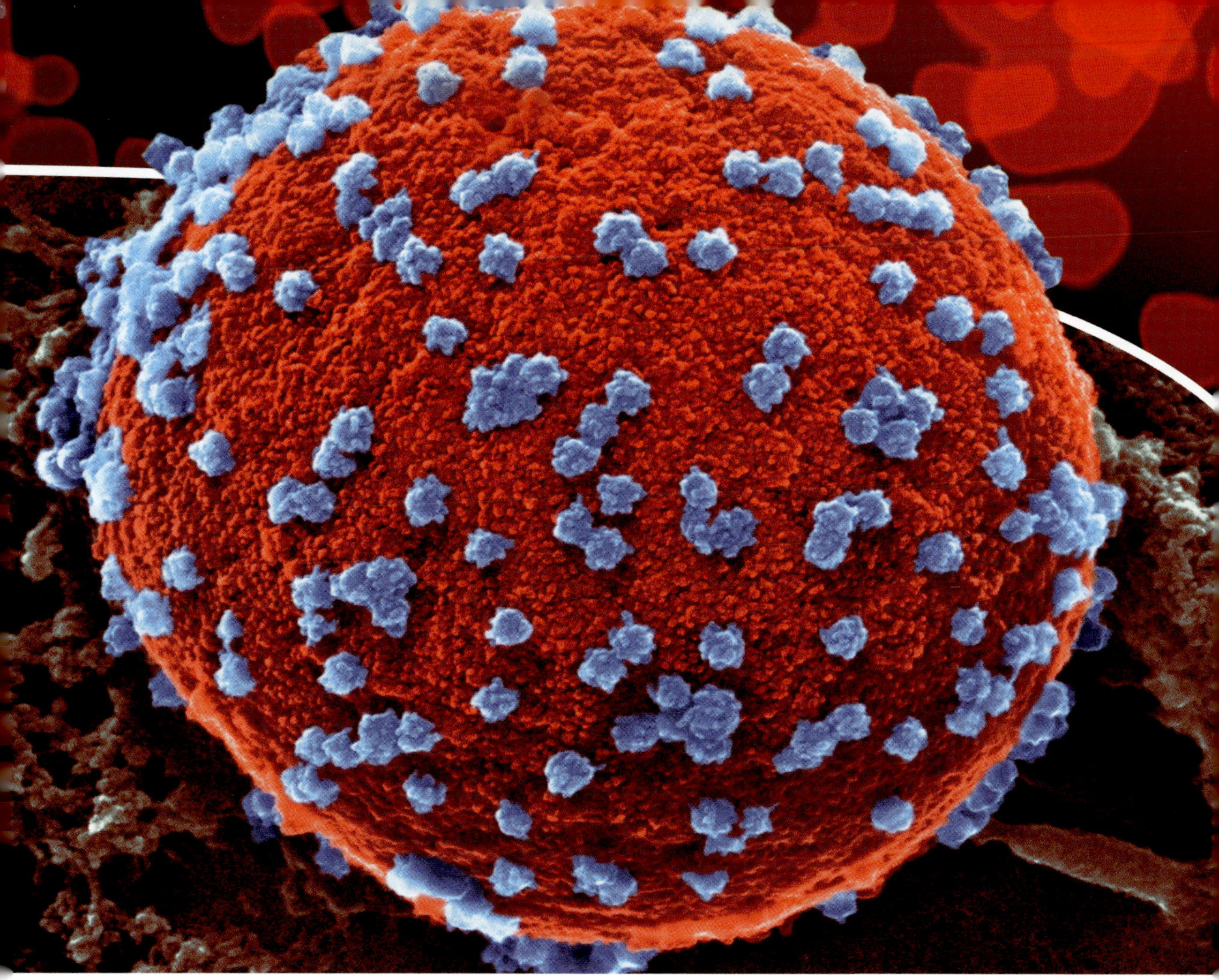

Take a Stand

Chapter Two describes responses to COVID-19. Some countries had severe lockdowns. Other countries did not. In the United States, states and cities made their own rules. Many people argued that lockdowns went against personal freedom. Imagine you are the leader of a country, state, or city. How would you have responded to the pandemic, and why?

GLOSSARY

chronic
long-lasting

contagious
able to spread from person to person

epidemic
a large increase in number of cases of a disease, spread over a large area

herd immunity
protecting a population by vaccinating most people to slow the spread of a disease

mutation
a change in the genetic structure of an organism

outbreak
a sudden rise in the occurrence of a disease

pandemic
a disease outbreak that spreads to many countries

transient
having people who stay or work for only a short time

vaccines
medicines that help a person's immune system prepare to fight a disease

ventilator
a medical device used to help people breathe

ONLINE RESOURCES

To learn more about COVID-19, visit our free resource websites below.

Core Library
CONNECTION
FREE! COMMON CORE MULTIMEDIA RESOURCES

Visit **abdocorelibrary.com** or scan this QR code for free Common Core resources for teachers and students, including vetted activities, multimedia, and booklinks, for deeper subject comprehension.

Booklinks
NONFICTION NETWORK
FREE! ONLINE NONFICTION RESOURCES

Visit **abdobooklinks.com** or scan this QR code for free additional online weblinks for further learning. These links are routinely monitored and updated to provide the most current information available.

LEARN MORE

Hustad, Douglas. *Understanding COVID-19*. Abdo, 2021.

London, Martha. *The Spread of COVID-19*. Abdo, 2021.

Moon, Walt K. *Past Pandemics and COVID-19*. BrightPoint, 2021.

INDEX

Centers for Disease Control and Prevention (CDC), 13, 32, 38, 41

discrimination, 17

face masks, 11, 13, 18, 20, 32

health-care workers, 12, 31, 36, 38
herd immunity, 36–37

influenza, 23, 24

lockdowns, 17, 33–34

mutations, 31, 38–39

online learning, 8, 12, 34
Operation Warp Speed (OWS), 37–38

remote work, 12, 34
RNA, 26

scientists, 15, 16, 21, 31, 38, 39–40
social distancing, 11, 13
spread of COVID-19, 7, 11–12, 15, 16–17, 39
symptoms, 9–11, 16–17, 27–29

treatments, 29, 34–36

vaccines, 19, 21, 32–33, 36–38, 39–40, 41
variants, 39

Wuhan, China, 16, 17–18

About the Author

Carol Hand has a PhD in zoology. She has taught college biology, written biology assessments, written middle and high school science curricula, and authored young-adult science books, including several on health-related topics. Currently she works as a freelance science writer.